Idle Fancies

poems

Joseph Hart

BBF, Johnny

Acknowledgments

Blue Unicorn: "Cats & Dogs," "Maxx," "Thanksgiving," "The candle smoke is rising"

The Pangolin Review: "Beauty," "Eliot"

Poetic Sun: "The Sea"

Raintown Review: "London"

Audience Magazine: "Keats' Picture," "A Picture on My Wall," "The Lake," "A Short Poem," "Temperate Love," "Romance," "Sleep & Love," "Ragged Lines," "Lines (Unforced sleep falls over me -)," "A Feeling," "The Three Graces"

Old Hickory Review: "Analogy"

Children, Churches & Daddies: "An Image"

Fauquier: "The Funeral," "Love," "Somewhere a cat"

Adept Press: "'Shine'"

Parnassus: "A Versicle from Keats"

Phenomenal Literature: "What is Chartres?"

Verbal Art: "Lines (My poems are a window on the night)"

Pegasus Review: "A Picture Found in an Old Book of Music"

Muse's Kiss: "A Fragment (I am cold, but not unkind)"

Romantics Quarterly: "The Ocean"

Poet's Roundtable: "I am a song without music"

Kaleidoscope Review: "A Poem Dreamt While Waking Up"

Vallum Magazine: "Stranded"

Contents

The candle smoke is rising

The candle smoke is rising
Through an infinite geometry,
And I am slowly yielding
To the guardian of sleep,
The soft caretaker, sleep.

London

The elder columns softly crack
And show their perfect age.
In the grey historical rain
Is Covent Garden, sage.
Around the irregular cobblestones
Grow flowers, limp and fair.
And through a tree
The breezes free
The music of the air.

"Shine"

I sit alone upon the beach.
Thalassic thunder rolls.
The ocean whispers to the fog,
"Madmen have no souls."

But if they do have hearts and souls
(In ruins and in tatters),
They wander by the sea and ask,
"Whatever really matters?"

Madmen are not brave,
But cowardly and wrong,
Seldom make much sense,
And are not loved for long.

Cats & Dogs

Dogs want love
But they slobber and drool.
Cats are loving
But nobody's fool.

Somewhere a cat

Somewhere a cat
Rubs its side against a fence.
That's sleep.
Cobwebs between doorless jambs
Are doors.
That's the moon.
Dark purple wine
Splashes down the sides
Of a lead mug.
That's the night.

Maxx

I'm different from my cat
And he is different from me.
It's happiness and love that give us
Similarity.

He sleeps across my arm.
I like to hear him purr.
Both of us will die
As if we never were.

The Prophet

She thought she was a prophet
And very very wise.
Every day she prayed
To something in the sky.

Then when she turned 70
She had to realize
That Jesus didn't answer
And even prophets die.

Fragment

If all throughout my soul I feel
A sweet, immortal tenderness,
And if my senses apprehend
The soft approach of earthbound sleep -

1970

Keats' Picture

My photograph of Keats
Is greasy with my kisses.
Could I assume
The spectre of his shape?
Passed time and through the grave
I reach into the past
And summon up the image of a ghost;
While the starry heavens twinkle
And the heavy, even waves
Heave their massive bulk upon the shore
And come toward my feet
Like withered leaves.

Analogy

I plunged a dagger
Through my hand,
Impaled it to the table
(An artifact
As natural as rocks);
And this, I said
Is my relationship
To all of nature.
And nothing other,
Nothing more remains.
And I am not
Nor ever can be free.
Would my sensations
Were my sentiments!

An Image

The subtle consternation of the sea,
The constant sea that sleepily engulfs
The sodden, deep-sunk posts of wooden piers
Is heaving its involvements to the sand.
The sky is low. Already I can feel
The nearness in an image
Of the deepness of the sea.
I see the sea in human conjuration.
Up from the depth I think the depth
Of oceans.
About the sea - I wonder what there is
About the sea; a magic I can touch
About the sea.

The Funeral

A muttered incantation,
A ritual said
Over the dead:
Then silence
That lay as still and smooth
As untrod snow,
Which seemed like a sleep without dreams -
So went the rite of passage,
The metamorphosis
From eyesight seeing
To unexpected darkness.
Gestures, mumbles, tears, beliefs,
And finally nothing evermore -
Forgetfulness was accepted
And forgotten.

Love

And dread, the feeling
Creeps over me
Like moss
Over the lips of a statue
That I am ridiculous.
But is it better
Never to look after my feelings?
Never to express love?
But rather to remain
Still and placid,
Noncommittal,
Like the surface of a pond
Whose water never
Ripples or splashes or breaks?

Beauty

Callas said music
Is meant to be soothing.
Keats wrote a beautiful song.
Integrity, talent are driven away
In a world where it's
Right to be wrong.

Thanksgiving

Thanksgiving for the turkeys -
Let turkeys ask the blessing,
Then gobble people down
With pumpkin pie and dressing.

The Sea

The ocean is an ugly thing.
You drown in its embrace.
From its depth you don't escape
In animal disgrace.

You like a sunken galleon sink
And settle in the silt,
Investigated by the fish,
Eyes closed. Do what thou wilt.

And as the currents carry you
Beneath the sea and far,
You are extinguished like a lamp,
And buried, like a star.

The Three Graces

(a painting in Earl Stine's guestroom)

The oak has split and acts as braces
For the flowers it displaces
And the three reclining Graces
Seated in their balanced posture
In this cool and blue-green cloister.
Rich and fragrant flowers wreathe them
And a river runs beneath them.
One watches her reflection
In still extro-introspection.
The other two relax conversing
While the morning sun is nursing
Deep wide shadows, blues and browns,
That slant across their milk-white gowns.
A sleep-sweet wakefulness they drink
Inside this human cove, I think.

1968

A Versicle from Keats

It is winter;
And the day is bare.
The birds peck about in the gravel
On my window ledge
Quickly, abrupt and alert
While I sit and watch them.
But it seems in fancy I
Am in the winter weather with them
Scratching at the pebbles -
In my imagination.

The Battle

Firing from the battlements
While all the soldiers slept,
Shooting at innumerable
Enemies that kept

Coming, just like roaches
Everywhere he stepped -
Finally he threw aside
His pistol and just wept.

Elizabeth

Elizabeth, Lizzie,
Betsy and Bess
All went to town
In the very same dress.
One said "no,"
One said "yes,"
One said "maybe,"
And one said "guess!"
Elizabeth, Lizzie,
Betsy and Bess,
Standing there wearing
The very same dress,
All of a sudden
Began to regress,
Which bothered the neighbors,
More or less.

A Picture Found in an Old Book of Music

Chiaroscuro cherubs in ensemble
Dance among the heather with their trumpets,
Clashing small grey cymbals in the silence
While night boils black and whitely from the heath.
A sylvan nymph stands near the lightening-roses
And blows her bleak recorder in the twilight.
Pale limp narcissus and warm edelweiss
Hang loosely in her shadow-hair. The moon
Drops pale and silver petals to a pool
That's unreflecting like a darkened mirror.
Four naked cherubs link their tiny hands
And dance a brief quadrille among the leaves.
The grass is darkness crushed. A rhythmed fog
Obscures the silent music of the scene.

1967

On the Sea

The rhythms were like swells that break
Into waves upon the sand
And flood the shore
With sibilance surrounding every rock,
Ere sliding back into the sea again.
The splashing breakers carried clams and shells,
Leaving them adrift
Among green seaweed on the dunes.
The ocean in a rush came to the shore,
Then quietly subsided back to sea.

A Fragment

I am cold, but not unkind,
Though caring, not demonstrative.
And now the rusted water pipes
Underneath the sink
Look sinister and sad.
Guilt and fear obsess me.
The colors on the walls accuse me,
And the chairs,
The pictures in their frames.

The Ocean

Opening as coves do on the ocean
That thunders on the walls inside the cave
In explosions of a foamy ecstasy,
A rhapsody of sound and splashing darkness,
Water slung up to the sea-soaked ceiling,
Higher caves of darkness and old time;
And each explosion makes a new explosion,
A rapture in a wet reverberation,
And then withdraws. The quietness seems sudden.
The floor of water swiftly swims away
Back out into the beckoning deep sea,
Like two wet hands of watery smooth grey
Withdrawn into the ocean, where again
Enlarging swells far out from the deep cavern
Roll in and break and hurl themselves in waves
Against the shore, far back into the caves,
There continuing this tireless repetition
As though they had some purpose to accomplish,
The maintenance of their identity.

A Picture on My Wall

The gnarled wind-wetted wooden posts
Point blindly to the sea,
Stuck in sand around the rocks
In rugged old complaisance.
The sea gulls crown the inner air
With swoops of flight and noises.
Their double-crescents, grey and white
Swim just above the swells.
The reef of rocks in silhouette
Rears ragged from the sea.
The taste of salt is in the sand,
The old posts slant and lean.
And all is blue and all is grey.
The ocean's deadly rustle
Washes up against the rocks
And then goes back to sea.
In the sky the subtle clouds
Are like the puffs of breath
Against a hand when someone speaks.
The wind is cool and warm.

I am a song without music

I am a song without music
Remembering what is forgotten,
Baffled and tender, a unicorn
Who is wholly self-conscious of sleep.
Give me a random explanation,
Anyone's understanding will do,
Or else the form of communication
I need to set me free,
Or hours more alone
To read the book of sleep.

A Poem Dreamt While Waking Up

I fall asleep easily
But wake up frequently
(Like a cat);
And there are little puddles of sleep
Scattered promiscuously
About the surfaces of my house.

The Lake

The still water's moving slightly
And the sun has planned a path
From its shiny center to my feet.
And I could step upon it
And walk out to the middle
And sink beneath the surface,
The cold appealing surface,
To the warm enclosing bottom
Of oblivion.

1963

Romance

A poem read by candlelight
In an empty castle
Cold but by the grating
In a small rock chamber,
Read to rhythms perfectly.
Allow the syllables
To make their music -
Pictures in the air
And humanistic phrases -
Narcissistic songs.

Temperate Love

Sleep not in sunlight too intense
Nor in the forest grimly dense
But in the shadow of a tree
With dark, warm, gentle light on thee
And all with no philosophy
But love and sad mortality.
And I shall lie with thee, my friend,
If thou dost want it til the end
Of daylight. Know the night with me
In sleep and gentle ecstasy.
Our passing thoughts we shall exchange.
No trait in thee will seem more strange
To me than those that are mine own.
And safer love we've never known.

1967

Sleep & Love

(Gary)

Half asleep you reached to hug me
Twice and said, "I love you too."
Tenderly to disencumber
Consciousness with gentle slumber,
Sleepy love is deeply true,
And I am in love with you.
Childish sleep can softly prove
The warm sincerity of love.

A Short Poem

Keats will outlive the sages
And their hells with his several pages
And their spells. Cziffra will endure
The ruins of years. His playing, rapid and sure,
More than his peers. However we will die,
My cats and I, be totally forgotten
By and by. Kindertoten
In sweet rhyme. And fortresses nook-shotten
Over time.

Lines

My poems are a window on the night,
If the window's ice and night is empty.
I'd rather be Millay or Johnny Keats.
Who am I? Or what? Personify
Nothingness. And that is poetry.
Though not with the indifference of a tomb.

My Cat

I pet my cat. He shuts his eyes,
In sleepy warm contentment lies.
In my house he's not a waif,
And thinks he is completely safe.
Precious cat, you make me cry.
You're no more secure than I.

Eliot

I see the skulls of death
In living faces.
I hear the ocean moan
From long ago.
Like human breath
That leaves its winter shadow
On the window,
Such is present sense.

Ragged Lines

The castle's circular towers
Arise to the ceiling, the sky.
The ruined tombs and the blasted trees
Emit a silent cry.
And death will come
As some unsummoned calm
To soothe away
The grief and the regrets.
The sea will smooth the sand,
And like a balm,
An anodyne – the ocean quite forgets
That would not remember anyway.
Upon the shore, my empty hand may find
A shell, a piece of coral
Or a stone
That eases or arouses all my mind.
To feel its edges,
Look upon its color,
To dream about a phantom or a skull or
A ghost that wafts about the chilly gloom
In the sleepy corner
Of a dim archaic room,
Musty lighted by a candle-lamp.
The tapestries are faded,
Old and damp.
The castle's solid, stoic,
Heavy, old.
A dim, medieval hymn exhales

With breath into the cold.
The castle stands upon a distant hill.
The air around me is so very still.
The turrets rise but do not touch the sky.
The ghosts are dead, so do not fear to die.
The stolid castle walls are very thick.
About the stout portcullis,
The wind is cool and quick.

1984

Lines

Unforced sleep falls over me -
A wave across the shore.
Comparing slumber to the sea!
A perfect metaphor!

Beneath the tide lie dreams and reefs
And hulls of sunken ships,
Forgotten loves and old beliefs
And unremembered lips.

Lines

God and evolution –
I thought they both were bats -
But if the universe has edges,
Why not fur on cats?

Or possibly a God -
Though indifferent to me -
The purring of a kitten,
Music, poetry -

A Feeling

Beneath the winter skies
I sit upon a rock beside the sea
That presages my incipient demise
And gives a sense of immortality.
And by sea I have been kissed
Upon my body, so my soul.
I feel cold bubbles in the mist,
And listen to the shoal.

Dining Out

In a quaint expensive restaurant,
With music most serene,
Sat several Martians dining
On very fine cuisine.

While eating appetizers,
A well-dressed Martian said,
"This person I am eating
Is not entirely dead!"
With manners quite impeccable,
He bit off its head.

A little squirt of blood
Trickled down his chin.
He wiped it off politely
(A moment of chagrin).

While Holding Maxx

Animals love,
Bur they die alone,
Every God
To them unknown.

Maxx will curl
In my coat and sleep.
This is a love
I cannot keep

Longer than life.
What can I do?
Do cats love God?
Cats are true.

Stranded

Evolution seems
So silly it's absurd -
The whiskers on a cat -
All the feathers on a bird.

And creationism's bogged
In such an awful mire
Of moral Christian fictions,
Bigotry and fire.

That leaves me where I'm standing
With nowhere left to go.
There's nothing to believe
And even less to know.

Lines

Nothing in the world is sane
But animals and music,
Or the columns toted up
In a dusty ledger -

And Horowitz whose music makes
A thousand thousand stars
Bursting through a cloudless night,
Illumining the sea -

What is Chartres?

What is Chartres? Is it a cathedral
Or the brief expression of a concept?
An old, abandon building is condemned.
On one crumbling wall I'll draw my face,
The dearest image and the oldest source,
A perfect likeness of mortality.

Peace

(my cat)

Maxx slept in my lap
For over half an hour.
While he did, a mood came over me.
I didn't know in nature
There was such a power
That heals –
But music or good poetry.

Paradoxes

Questions without answers
Decaying in old graves -
The universe has edges -
Light is particles and waves.

The waking dream of madness
Comes somehow from your mother.
This life was unexpected;
So why not another?

Lines

Mystics, saints and madmen
Thinking they know why
See more than stars and music
In the sky.

Traveling and traveling,
Not going very far -
All the stones in Christendom
Do not make a star.

The Rhinoceros

I saw a picture of a man -
Dark complected, sad -
His forehead on the face
Of a dead rhinoceros -
Everything will die -
And some things love -

Thought In Childhood

Life is like an onion.
You peel away a layer
And there's another layer.
And when you peel them all away,
There's nothing there at all.

Lines

I just watched a cop
Dancing in the street
With a little Black kid.
Watching it was sweet.
Affection is a thing
Hate cannot defeat.